I0449234

AMANDLA!

[A SHORT SURVEY OF STUDENT ACTIVISM IN LIBERIA]

AMANDLA!

[A SHORT SURVEY OF STUDENT ACTIVISM IN LIBERIA]

K-Moses Nagbe, PhD

Amandla!
A Short Survey of Student Activism in Liberia

Published by the Pentina Publishers, Inc.

Maryland, USA
Monrovia, Liberia

© K-Moses Nagbe 2023

All rights reserved. No part of this book may be reproduced, stored in retrieval system, or transmitted by any means, electronic, mechanical, photocopying, recording or otherwise, without written permission from the author and the publisher.

ISBN: 978-1-312-59612-2

Formatted by pen2publish, India
Printed at Lulu, USA

Send inquiries to kateabela@gmail.com

Amandla: The title is South African, the full reading being "Amandla Ngawethu," a Zulu expression meaning power to the people. Or, the power is ours – people's power. Used in Liberia because of its popularity. Of course, that's African as well!

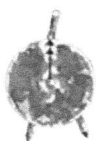

We make cheap
Many drink deep

This Book Is Dedicated to

People in the Trenches
to Make Life a Little Better
for the Ordinary Man,
Woman, and Child
Everywhere

Introduction

IN MARCH 2023, THE LIBERIAN social media platforms flashed ablaze with a spate of riotous scenes at the University of Liberia, particularly on the Capitol Hill campus. Many members of the Student Unification Party were caught up in chants and denunciations, countered by PROSA, a student group apparently vested in promoting the George Weah-led government and its numerous functionaries. How many mushrooming student groups has poor University of Liberia not seen!—ASAP, SIM, STUDA, and the list goes on.[1] A CDC-leaning Member of the House of Representatives[2] was scheduled to visit the University, purportedly, to hold a luncheon with students under his sponsorship. There were antecedent incidents of tension on the University's Capitol Hill campus. First, the Vice President of the nation had been reportedly jeered at. Second, a past government official, the Solicitor General, had also been heckled, with projectiles flung at his vehicle. In either case, the rationale had been that any official of government with a less than stellar public service performance record deserved the wrath of the student body or a part thereof.

Now, set for the presumed luncheon, the lawmaker took along a slew of security detail, and when he arrived on campus, the security sprang on many of the protesting students, mishandling some of them, including some press personnel, until at one end, someone began to shout: "Aey, Aey, that's a pressman, a pressman![3] As a past student activist—although never a fiery type—I realized several related scenes of yesteryears crawling through my head. It would seem that until we are dead, our past never ceases to trail us. The human mind seems borderless. The scenes led me to wonder: Was that how we did it? The chants I could recognize. The fiery language, minus vituperations, I could recognize. But the authentic, running battle of projectiles? That seemed an addition, a disturbing addition. Concededly, when disconcerting practices in society spiral upwards with ugly increment and intensity, one needs to be a little more depressed.

Prior to these March 13 scenes, I'd been wrestling with the idea of producing a serious book focusing specifically on student activism in Liberia. I'd captured a few vignettes in my previous works, including *Between the Scissors: Growing Up as an Afrestern Liberian*, *My Compatriot, Your Compatriot: Surveying Forces and Voices That Inspired the Union of Liberian Associations in the Americas*, *April Fourteen*, and *One Saturday in August*, the latter being a novel. These books captured basically the energy confluence of youth and adults in Liberia, but I wanted to do things a little differently, to provide solely the Liberian experience of youth/student activism. However import-ant the confluence of youth and adult engagement may seem, I often wanted a time to decouple the energies. The closer one looks at a specific thing, the clearer it becomes.

I'd tried a title framed as "When Fangs Meet Fangs: Understanding the Contours of Student Activism and National Development." Fundamentally, it was my way of comparing youth/student rage vis-à-vis government's sometimes ruthless response, such as when beasts in a fight bare their fiendish teeth. The canine and the feline families do that in serious brawls or battles. The point is that generally when rage descends among human beings, with eyes stretching as if to roll out of sockets, the mouths wide open and foaming at the corners, mouth muscles receding, neck veins bulging, arms sweating and stretch-ing, veins bulging, fingers forming fists to relay the inten-sity of the rage, followed by the occasional or persistent pelting match of projectiles, there is no way that you capable of the relevant words cannot capture or paint, even if cryptically or succinctly, the human drama that often unfolds in demand of urgent needs, beckoning the requisite response without which some ultimate calami-tous end, perhaps in the form of dark plumes of smoke, engulfs the land.

My core intention in using that title of fangs facing fangs was to draw attention to (1) the gap in national conversation regarding the place of student activism, (2) the importance of that missing student link in the conversation about national development in Liberia, (3) the energy of student activism in driving national development, and (4) how Liberian students have done it.

If the education of young people needs to be taken seriously, their role in national development, much of a youth-centered or student-centered focus, needs equal significant attention. But it seemed that the title—fangs facing fangs—as framed was sensational. I heard that some colleagues, a part of the "lord guardians" of abstracts, fussed under-breath about the hue of the title. I would not blame them. Doctoral studies, especially the path toward restive research, infuse students with the attributes of scientificness, one of which is to remain objective at all costs. We are encouraged to eschew the melodramatic. Science should not thrive on melodramatic language. Science needs to emphasize seriousness. With that seriousness, or the appearance thereof, comes enormous public or private attention and support, material as well as financial.

I have heard all that. I have imbibed much of that. Nevertheless, I often tell these colleagues—those who are *au courant* with the biting pressure of doctoral — studies—that graduation is liberating. In school, protocols demand that students follow learning frames and scaffolds that have come down the ages because they have been tried and tested. Conservatism, which is the suggestive professional mold of all these protocols, has its place in life. Yet, with progressivism, the spirit of flexibility, and the spirit of finding a dozen other ways beckoning, someday such orthodox frames and scaffolds might be dismantled.

Until then, a student should oblige. But in the real world, there is ample evidence that even science sometimes eschews orthodoxy; science is really not stagnant. This reality stamps the rationale for unabated research programs and projects. It leads to another reality that some old theories as well as old conclusions continue to undergo reinvestigation and reveal new conclusions. We have always heard, "Scientists thought that this was so and so, but new studies have compelled us to draw new conclusions." This is true when it comes to the causations of certain diseases, the composition and functions of interplanetary systems, and even about topics related to the very human body which throughout the years medical practitioners thought they had fully captured and conquered. Nothing about life and Nature seems stuck in cement.

Understandably, I simply have to try out a plethora of styles and strategies to get any message of mine across, making sure of verifiability. That is to say, if what I say is true, the vindication is rewarding; it would not matter whatever color of language I use. Remember that in such matters of trying out new ways, I draw from a multidisciplinary wealth of knowledge, part of which is media and literature. As a media and literary person, I know quite well that where bland titles or messages, in the name of sounding scientific, will not foist my core conclusion through steel heads, I will darned well use a language, minus vituperations, that will perforate the heart, which often is the seat of human emotions.[4]

Certainly, that was how I used one other title framed as, "The Crucifixion of Snobbery: Critical and Enduring Lessons from Election 2017" for a *Liberian Studies Journal* article.[5] The work in that journal article evolved from my book, *The Scum of the Earth: How They Bonded and Incensed the Economic Tribe of Liberia in Election* 2017. Styles and strategies are like trademarks. Where they jell, let the well flow!

Today, I have mustered sufficient energy to begin the personally long-sought project on student activism and national development. I plan to make this initial effort a teaser, an appetizer. That is to say, I plan on purpose to make the work very short, something to be read in one sitting. I am relieved.

The work, although short, has multiple parts. It has six chapters. Chapter One looks at the varied shades of what it means to be a young person or student—I'll use both words interchangeably. Chapter Two focuses on both the African and the Liberian youth and student in the context of the pre- and post-arrival of Western and sundry cultures. Chapter Three looks at the dynamics of the energy which has evolved from the surge of cultural merger and configuration. Chapter Four talks about the theatre of rebellion, examining how the energy from youthful activism has played out, and how it has impacted national development, even if implicitly. Chapter Five runs a survey of state response to student activism. Chapter Six lays out briefly the accumulated lessons drawn from student activism and national development. Each chapter is followed by notes, and then there is a body of references.

This work is a part of my contribution to conversations related to national as well as human development through paying attention to multiple voices without which progress may cease or be less impressive. Again, as a starter, I have made this volume of conversation, youth-focused and especially short—to increase interest and circulation in the subject.

K-Moses Nagbe, PhD
Maryland, USA
March 2023

Introduction: Notes

[1]ASAP: All Students Alliance Party; SIM: Student Integration Movement; STUDA: Student Democratic Alliance.

[2]That lawmaker was Alcarus M. Gray of the Coalition for Democratic Change (CDC), which at the time was the ruling coalition.

[3]Regarding the screaming call to save the journalist, see footage of the Diaspora TV platform known as Focus on Liberia owned by Dennis Jah and others in Atlanta, Georgia. At the time, Prince Mulbah was the newscaster on call.

[4]When I think about the coloration of language, I think of William Zinsser who, in his *On Writing Well*, encourages attention to one's language intended to win readers over, not necessarily to be flippant but to entertain in a way to ensure absorption of the embedded message. There is also Steve Evans whose recognition of the power of storytelling to enrich one's understanding of a situation appeals to me. His "The Impact of Cultural Folklore on National Values: A Preliminary Study with a Focus on

Bhutan," at https://www.jstor.org/stable/41949037?item_view=read_online, remains insightful in the matter.

[5]For that "Crucifixion of Snobbery" article, see the *Liberian Studies Journal*, 44 (1 & 2), 2019.

Table of Contents

The Varying Shades of Students

The Youth as Student

ALTHOUGH THE WORD "STUDENT" HAS come to span the ages of youth and adults, most often than not, the word evokes the population of young people. Words are susceptible to times and circumstances. Perhaps, the concept of student has trodden from the chronological circumstances of human evolution, inviting physiological markers and mental abilities to understand what goes on in life. Thus, in the basic, binary, and chronological structure, where the first part of life focuses on training and readiness, while the second part focuses on maturity and service to society, we tend to look at that primary part as the moment of training and readiness and the secondary part as the moment of service to society. To that primary part, for this book, I affix the more applied meaning of the word "student."

Yet, looking at the word in its most technical and fluid definition, it encompasses the whole range of ages and protocols of learning; that is, it has to do with being positioned at any time for absorbing new information. In that context, everybody, young or old, will at one time or another stand in the need of information. Life being what it is, no one human being has all information in the world at one single moment or time. We learn as we travel through life. No wonder it is often said that "learning never ends."

But for the sake of the initial, critical part of this book, let's use the operational definition of student as *one who, prior to arriving at the peak in life to engage in crucial service to society, needs some requisite training and expertise.* The key phrase is "to engage in crucial service." This stage requires sound decision-making protocols. It requires critical thinking skills. It requires a deep understanding of the relationship between actions and consequences. It requires the use and understanding of critical interpersonal or people skills.

Youth: The Matter of Innocence and Inexperience

STUDIES IN CHILD Psychology and Early Childhood Education invite us to understand the ranges of life, or at least the start of life. We move from infant to toddler, and then to at least adolescence. This is the most vulnerable stage of human beings where human needs, including cradling, feeding, and nurturing remain crucial. This is the stage that clarifies our early beginnings as we enter the space known as life. Thinkers, such as Jean Jacques Rousseau, Jean Piaget, and Erik Erikson, remind us of how blank our brains are, like a slate, at the beginning of life. That stage is described as the stage of innocence and inexperience. This is here that a child can become impressionable or gullible. In other words, the child may be vulnerable to accepting things that seem true or real. Here, at this stage of innocence and inexperience, we remain until gradually prints begin to appear as we engage with individual environments populated with our parents, our community, and so on, as Urie Bronfenbrenner reminds us.[1]

These prints are manifested in what we see, what we feel, what we hear, what we taste, and what we smell. That is why at the beginning of cognition, the lessons of awareness include knowing about the five human senses—the sense of sight, sense of touch, sense of hearing, sense of taste, and the sense of smell.

Imagine an empty room. There is no floormat. There is no bed. There is no mirror. There are no chairs. There are no racks for clothes and shoes. There is no television or radio. Over time, things that were not present begin to come in. Soon, the room is filled. Think of the empty room as the human mind prior to all things crowding in. Once these things enter the room and you are aware of them, you obviously begin to place them in proper order. Next, you begin to explore their meaning and their significance.

Youth: The Matter of Idealism

AT THE EARLY stage of life, our world seems to be filled with big ideas. It is filled with dreams about what we want to be, what we want to do, what we want to see, where we want to be, and where we want to go. It is all about our expectations. It suggests the image of the unhindered flow of a body of water. And then, a log or a wall gets in the way, forcing the flow to change course. Wanting to follow a certain course of movement but being denied that course of movement leads to a certain level of tension. That tension is characterized as conflict. It is all about the phenomenon of desiring to do one thing, yet being denied the space or the opportunity of doing that thing. The concept of conflict is the concept of rupture in human relationships, for example. It has trailed human existence.

When conflict occurs, the need for resolving the rupture arrives in order that the phenomenon of flowing without hindrance reappears. Yet, the reality in life is that certain flows meet their points or moments of disruption or termination because of unavoidable reasons. It may be that the flow meets an intersection that simply has to exist. The dynamics of life often produce a multiplicity of intersectionality that ought to be understood for useful coexistence. Life is sometimes diminished by the poverty of absolute freedom. The faster we understand that reality, the more enjoyable operating in life's limitations becomes. The poverty of absolute freedom takes almost a lifetime to be understood. It takes enormous and sometimes vexing rounds of experience for people to understand that unless we recognize intersectionality and interdependence, we cannot sustain our very own individual lives. We simply have to oblige.

Experience is the restraint on idealism. Idealism has to do with someone existing in a space populated with ideas. In that context, I always think of a time when a child has a can or a jar filled with liquid soap and a plastic ring with a handle. Every now and then, the child dips the ring and handle in the liquid and blows through the ring. Each time it is done, a bubble flies out, then another, and another. Each bubble floats for a while and explodes. The game of bubbles continues until the liquid soap is all gone. Each bubble represents an idea. Except simply to watch the bubble float, nothing else can one do with the bubble.

Similarly, our minds come up with multiple ideas. We may find means of making the ideas come alive, as when we think about building a chair for someone to sit in. We will need planks, glue, nails, and a saw. These things working together, we end up bringing to live something that was just an idea. Thus, we can say, an idea is soil from which a plant may grow. This is just a comparison. That soil may be compared to wishing to go to school to get a skill, getting a skill to make some money, making some money to buy some food, etc. When you've acquired a skill, made some money, and bought whatever thing of desire, then, clearly, the plant has grown!

If we dream of making a chair but do not have what it takes to get the planks, glue, nails, and a saw, the dream will simply stay in the condition of being an idea. Until we know definitely that it takes something else, something like money, to get the materials, we stand to be frustrated. Knowledge, which is a form of experience, will remind us that something requires something to become something.

Experience is the string by which idealism is tacked and anchored. Yet, Nature has the luxury of slowly infusing experience into the human species. And what, really, is the term "experience" by the way? Among multiple definitions, one is likely to understand that experience is a psychophysical or metaphysical phenomenon. The following definition may be useful: Experience "is a light or the opportunity that Fate offers an individual or a group to face up to a future problem."[2] This means that if an individual has not seen that light or acquired that opportunity, the problem that presents itself in the future cannot be easily or comfortably addressed.

The difference between youthhood and adulthood is a gulf, a dangerous gulf. That gulf translates as time. Youths, by increments of time, need to absorb modicums of experience that will often help with navigating the various problems or tests that life offers in the future—tests related to varied scenes of human relationships, tests related to how to find food and feed oneself, tests related to how to approach dangers to avoid illness and death, tests related to how to remain on top of things as long as living is possible.

Youth: The Matter of Rebellion

YET, THE GULF between youthhood and adulthood is an interregnum that can be tragic. It can capture momentous feistiness between a population that is impatient to await the apex of growth and a population that is intolerant of anyone ignorantly or willfully disrespecting the height of age and its sundry perks. Achievement is often precious. Whoever easily accepts disrespect for one's achievements! That feistiness between impatience and intolerance is rebellion. Now, there often are varied reasons for rebellion. There may be a rebellion to right a wrong. There may be a rebellion to wall off a wrong. There may be a rebellion as an act of mischief, a sort of tantrum.

Rebellion as a tantrum is the worst form because of its mindlessness, its depths and widths of destruction, and its sometimes immeasurable economic toll on a community, an institution, or an entire society. Whatever the nature of a rebellion, the knowledge of its causation and consequences must be fully or significantly fused into the decision that originates it and drives it. To be oblivious or to be insensitive to any or both causation and consequences calls to question the concept of growth and cognition.

Rebellion is a gateway to unpleasant acts of human beings. Rebellion is a manifestation of rage, momentary or prolonged insanity, which is a period wherein human beings take on debased qualities of destruction and murder. The more the deficit of experience, the more virulent and adversely impactful a rebellion can become. After all, it is experience, as said earlier, that helps human beings restrain themselves from the extremes of any actions bent on ruination.

Maturity: When Youth and Adult Part Ways, or Do They?

MATURITY BECOMES THE border post of growth. It is here cognition takes place or achieves solidity—the capacity to understand fully or significantly not only what is right and wrong but also the consequences of each right act and each wrong act. Humanity realizes that at maturity every human being should be held responsible for whatever personal action that is committed. Of course, there may be a latitude regarding the grades of actions and the requisite penalties. Many configurations of actions, reactions, and penalties are possible as one moves from one society to another. Life is often intricate; it is multilayered.

Indeed, at maturity, youthhood and adulthood seem to part ways. But the delineation or the dichotomy is not as clinical or mechanical as it may seem. Circumstances and vulnerabilities of humanity are varied and vast. If the statement—"All humans are susceptible to times and circumstances"—is any truth to accept, then vulnerabilities that elevate our emotional shades of anger, sorrow, envy, etc. are the fundamental rationale for the susceptibility. These shades never easily grow old. They often swing like a pendulum between our young fragile selves and our old deceptively sturdy selves. One circumstance that may seem trivial at one time may be monumental at another time, given particular times and circumstances.

Chapter One: Notes

[1]Urie Bronfenbrenner's Ecological Systems Theory suggests a five-cycle support system for each child to become a full, serviceable human being.

[2]For this Fate-related definition of "experience," see p. 162 of Nagbe's *Beyond Buffoonery: Exploring Ways to Get Liberia Well-Rooted in All Things Diligent and Dignifying*.

CHAPTER TWO

The African Youth

CULTURE—THE CONFIGURATION OF WAYS, purposes, and entreaties in life pursued by individuals and groups—provides variations about how to approach youthhood, and that understanding applies to studenthood. It also applies to geographical locations, in terms of whether one is talking about rural life or urban life. At the basic level, rural life responds to life predominantly unaided by machines, whereas urban life responds to life predominantly aided by machines. A machine, we need to remember, is that which provides succor to muscular energy.

The rural child works largely with limbs and a creative mind, feeding off whatever generated natural product. The urban child's situation is not so. From the bicycle or car available to move from one point to another to the numerous mechanical gadgets to gather and prepare food, that child lives a life that spells a life of paradise, if by paradise we understand a life of ease, comfort, and laughter. Of course, times continue to change gradually. In about the past 50 or 100 years, rural regions of the past may not look like rural regions of today. A few aids to ameliorate the harsh realities of life have appeared in rural regions. There are abundant clothing and footwear, at least transistor radios, if not televisions, better shelters, etc. These have come with the increase in transport and communication technology. After all, with such technology floats an abundance of cultural ideas.

Considering the circumstances created in the life of the rural child and the life of the urban child, how each child grows and the parental expectations developed may vary. It bears adding that the rural child in developed countries and the one in developing countries may be vastly different. That is true of children in urban areas of the developed world and those in the developing world. Those in developed countries would fare better than those in the developing world.

An understanding of the foregoing life situations in the cultural and geographical areas as a preface will hopefully clarify expectations of the context of youthhood and studenthood in which the current discussion is interested.

Wherever you may live or may have been born, it is clear that human beings are a little notch above lower animals. Instead of a lower animal that needs a day or two and is expected to begin at least the first phase of life which is ambulation, human beings have a comparatively longer time for ambulation and sundry activities. Again, we are expected to live life as an infant, a toddler, an adolescent, etc. That is true, regardless of being in a developing or developed country. This means, then, that we all initially need cradling, feeding, and nurturing.

Until organized, intercultural or global, and intense learning systems evolved, the rural child in Africa, for example, was preoccupied with a particularized cubical or silo of cultural instructions—how to take care of the home and the community, how to identify and resolve intra- and intercultural and community conflicts, and how to guide and protect life. To evolve protocols for infusing cultural knowledge and skills, cultures established informal and formal institutions guided mainly by those who had earlier acquired the cultural knowledge and skills, thus, the shibboleth: "One who leads must've been led," or simply, "One who'd left chaperons incomers."

It may be clear, then, that the role of infusing cultural knowledge and skills, or imparting lessons, resided earlier and significantly with the elders of a cultural group as they served as cultural repositories. Until the advent of literacy, which provided a respite for rote, learning and lessons rested solely with human memory, and elders reigned supreme. No wonder it was often said that the death of an elder was the loss of a storehouse of tradition, or better still, "The loss of an elder is the loss of a storehouse of wisdom." Thus, the place of elders remained sacrosanct. This meant that one generation remained obeisant to a preceding generation. That order of existence and living protocols remained a given. None ignored that with impunity.

In the distant past, the African youth followed that order of existence and living protocols without fail. The young child grew up playing and learning from the older ones. If a girl, the practice was to bond with the mother and mother persona. If a boy, the practice was to bond with the father or father persona. This pattern of emulation became useful in the context of the cultural path and means of production. Farmers followed the tradition of farming. Herders followed the tradition of herding. That was true also of fishing. That was true also of the knowledge, skill, and dispensation of herbs. The order and protocols laid out the path of paternity and maternity, and then the path to adulthood. It moved initially from the moment of the first cry at birth to the first drop of the mother's milk and the taste of the first morsel of a solid meal. Cradling began. Crawling came in. Rising and falling followed, and then real toddling.

Soon, the counting of years, instead of months, began. Between 13 and 15 years,[1] that child graduated from the proprietary realm of the family to the communal realm. Here, the real contemplation of future meaning and worth rose. Here, lessons in folkways, mores, taboos, and laws[2] began. One cycle following another, life progressed along that path. For the African, for example, the preliminaries including scarification and some peel-offs[3] were begun. And by that time, the first phase of the protracted learning or the rite of passage that set in was completed at the top of the early teen years, which may be around age 15.

In cultures where both boys and girls obtained incisions, such was done. In other cultures where only boys received the cuts, that was done. This is all about the concept of male and female circumcision—if you want to know.

The Liberian Youth

FROM ITS EVOLUTION as a nation-state, meaning an arrangement of a socio-cultural and politico-legal merger, Liberia, in West Africa, has experienced a binary formation—indigenous and Western-flavored. Its indigenous populations, often referred to severally as "aborigines," "natives," or "country people," trekked from episodic eras dating to the fall of African kingdoms,[4] whereas its Western-flavored populations, those referred to severally as "settlers," "pioneers," "Americo-Liberians, or the Congoes" emerged from the post-slavery era dating to the early 1800s. These populations were offspring of victims of the well-known, traumatic, and tragic Atlantic Slave Trade that spanned from 1492 to the late 1700s.

The indigenous populations brought along their varied forms of socialization, some subscribing to methods of initiation that included scarification. Those, especially up north and central of present-day Liberia, used multiple aspects of scarification. Those, both in the south and east, were scant in the use of scarification. Many in the Kwa, for example, used particularly the forehead cicatrice and might apply marks to the forearms, the chest, and the lower back mainly as a form of vaccination or mystical protection. In the Mel and the Mande, one likely saw numerous individuals with the back, the forearm, and the chest populated with a generous spread of scarification.[5] These marks became the foundation and affirmation of both individual identity and particularized cultural knowledge and skills. These contextualized the moments in which lessons of the folkways, mores, taboos, and laws of individual cultural groups were usually dispensed.

Of course, when the Western-flavored populations arrived on the Grain Coast, they emerged with a system of organized, intercultural or global, and intense learning, which has gone by a few names—e.g., Western education or universal learning protocols, etc. Both the indigenous and the Western populations grafting to each other, howbeit involuntarily, with the latter predominating, there became a paradigm shift in learning protocols. Literacy as a purveyor of learning took center stage. The role of elders as the single dispenser of learning receded. Now, elders ordinarily are recognized not only by the wealth of knowledge and skill sets they hold, but also by their physical appearance—e.g., furrowed skin, hair coloration bent toward gray, and, in some instances, the beard, the mannerisms, the walking cane, etc. Such an appearance signals the sway they are likely to hold when they are met the first time.

Chapter Two: Notes

[1]While the years may begin with a teen base of 13, other societies go a year lower to 12. Might it have to do with the demands of youth work at a much earlier age where life expectancy is short? It probably is. In societies of longer life expectancy, there may not be a rush for children to be children.

[2]Drawing on the ideas of sociologists Chris Drew and Ashley Crossman, the snapshots of folkways, taboos, mores, and laws are as follows: *Folkways*—simple unwritten socially acceptable ways which people learn through intuition; *taboos*—social ways people find offensive or inappropriate when done; *mores*—ways somewhat linked to religious urgings that spell moral principles of life; *laws*—ways written to be followed by every inhabitant in a society. The breaking of each results in specific penalties.

[3]Olméta Quenum has an interesting article on scarification and sundry practices. You want to read "African Traditions and Customs: Scarification as a mark of cultural identity," https://www.afro-impact.com/en/african-traditions-and-customs-scarification-as-a-mark-of-cultural-identity/

[4]The basic list of such kingdoms includes Mali, Ghana, and Songhai in West Africa.

[5]In regard to the three linguistic groups, the *Kwa* include Kru, Grebo, Krahn, Belleh, Dey, and Bassa; the *Mel* include Gola and Kissi; and the *Mande* include Vai, Mende, Mandingo, Gbandi, Kpelle, Lorma, Mah (Mano), and Dan (Gio).

CHAPTER THREE

The Energy of Cultural Confluence

CONFIGURATION SUGGESTS PARTS, THE ARRANGEMENT of parts. It then goes without saying that there may be an element of fusion, the coming together of the parts of a system. As regards culture, while there may be a reference to the elements of just one culture, in a society of cultural diversity, as in speaking about the existence of a nation-state, one needs to be thinking about a confluence of cultures. The world today pays attention to that confluence, particularly with the advent of transport technology and communication technology driving the cris-crossing of ideas and people's lifestyles.

In the 1700s, when the Industrial Revolution showed its face in increments, there was the gradual realization that humanity would never be the same again.[1] Add the earlier story of the invention of writing in about 3500 BCE traced to the Sumerians and, later, to other claimers to that fame of progress—the Mayans, and the Chinese.[2] To be sure, the history of inventions can be a murky business, the farther back in time of a specific action. If records did not fly about in a given time, as they do now, claims, when time doesn't permit, easily pile up, overlapping as much as possible. In any case, the Sumerians tend easily to leap ahead on the list of inventors—or maybe it depends on who is speaking or writing about a specific invention.

The core point from this kernel of history is that besides the Industrial Revolution and the advent of transport and communication technology, the invention of writing discounted forever the proprietary character of thinking, thoughts, and ideas. Cultures, the crucible of thinking, thoughts, and ideas, would cyclically inject new blood into human activities. Thus, in Africa, and specifically Liberia, a monolithic perspective on distinct ways of life pursued by one cultural group or another would be shredded, if not merged. The life of farming, herding, fishing, and natural herbal treatment and protocols, shepherded by feisty guardians of the culture, would be intruded upon, relaxed, or terminated, trashed as being unhealthy, savage, or heathen. To defame or to denigrate is to silence.

Be that as it may, in Africa, and Liberia, the phenomenon of the confluence of cultures—Western and African—emerged, and with it the transformed attitudes, mannerisms, and behaviors of young people. Here, we must go back to the passing of time, and with that, the importance of dialogues and conversations, all of which center on the exchange of ideas as the driving engine toward human progress. In human history, persistent travel to find and inhabit vast land inspired conformity and collectivism in order to sustain one purpose and goal. Yet, for every period, endpoints are never irrelevant. Diseases and other pestilences, climatic conditions, anger, rage, and wars took their own tolls, driving the energy of moving from one space to another. We are as permanent as the forces and voices over which we have permanent control. Over time, a slew of marked mishaps that could have been avoided if dialogues and conversations preceded individual legs of progress necessitated the role of dialogues and conversations; dialogues and conversations were highlighted and elevated. Soon, conformity, the sole need for progress, gave way to inquiry, the ingredient of self-reliance and independence, the reality of polyvocal interactions—more drivers of progress. The tension between collectivism and individuality was born. It became the tension that would remain the central force, the energy of the configuration and confluence of cultures even in Africa and specifically in Liberia.

What did this configuration and confluence of cultures introduce? They introduced the cross-pollination of ideas. They clarified and exacerbated the natural tension between conservatism, the old, feisty order of thinking, and progressivism, the new, indulgent order of thinking. They inevitably created a phenomenon of osmosis of ideas, the spontaneous flow of ideas, from one side to another.

They increased the natural layers of rebellion, basically the phenomenon of standoffs or clashes to ensure an individual or group position of comfort. One cannot complete the discussion of the character of youth without commenting on the concept of rebellion and activism, which fundamentally are synonyms as we shall see more of. The first one or two chapters of this short work do provide an eye-opener on the subject. Where idealism, the desire, in a sense, to float or swim through dreams unhindered through time and space, exists, the seeds of rebellion are ripe to be sown.

Chapter Three: Notes

[1]For a little more on the industrial revolution, you want to read "Industrial Revolution: Definition, History, Dates, and Summary," at https://www.britannica.com/event/Industrial-Revolution

[2]*Encyclopedia Britannica* has an interesting article on the invention of writing titled, "Writing - History of Writing Systems," at https://www.britannica.com/topic/writing/History-of-writing-systems

CHAPTER FOUR

The Theatre of Rebellion

REBELLION IS THE RUPTURE THAT springs from the craving for unrestrained freedom; sometimes it is shadowed by the craving for equality. Rebellion shows its fiery head at the threshold of life. The nascent craving for personal independence sets the ball rolling. From when we begin moving our limbs actively and voluntarily, which is by the end of year one, moving into year two of life, as child development literature intimates, rebellion, even in its non-threatening or soft form, begins to show signals. As I see it, the fundamental desires of humanity, which comprise the linchpin of rebellion, may be enumerated as (1) the desire to move about unrestrained, (2) the desire to think unhindered, (3) the desire to live in comfort unhindered, including feeding and shelter, and (5) the desire to worship or not to worship.

Really, these match the numerous individual and group needs that constitutions around the world have captured in their preambles and promised to deliver. In some societies, they are marked as freedom of speech, freedom of the press, freedom of assembly, freedom of demonstrating to articulate discontent over distasteful policies, and freedom of petitioning leaders.[1] The list of freedoms really grows with the expansion of populations, times, and circumstances. Expansion is usually the enemy of freedom; it feeds the fire of rebellion. In substance, social, educational, economic, political, and religious issues have given rise to the drama of rebellion.

The point needs to be made here that rebellion goes by numerous names and terms. Here is a short list: activism, advocacy, protestation, radicalism, and revolution. Each term evolves, ushering its set of nuances. The human mind is so proprietary and territorial in such a way that if it has to create a particularized vocabulary to sound new and different, that is what its owner will pursue. We are captives of our own egos. In any case, the rudimentary watchword regarding the nuances of rebellion is that of destruction or damage, absent a personally preferred way of life. That is to say, to what extent does the specific standoff—our earlier succinct definition of rebellion—disrupt, damage, or destroy normalcy in society?

In Africa, and in the distant past, prior to the advent of other cultures, the obvious natural desire for comfort in life created episodic skirmishes. That was rebellion, whether soft or hard. Whether one spoke of a society of young or old, rich or poor, strong or weak, such skirmishes were inevitable. Among human beings, competing self-interests are never without moments of serious contestation. However, the utmost need for collectivism, conformity, and, in essence, peace, seemed to reign supreme. Using a panoply of conflict management strategies—e.g., the use of peer groups, lineage elders, sodalities, spiritual agents, etc.—whatever rebellion that was emerging was often contained, and life moved on.

But we must return to the subject of focus in this book—the young person, the student, and the needed role in national development. Prior to the entry of Western culture into Africa, collectivism and conformity enjoyed a heyday. Respect for adulthood and elders enjoyed enormous respect. A young person needed simply to listen to the wishes and advice of the elders and things would presumably go well. In Liberia, West Africa, even when the Western-flavored Africans landed on the continent, elders on both sides enjoyed respect from the young people because indigenous or Western-flavored, elders expected and treasured respect from young people. It would not take long comparatively when instances of disparity between indigenes and WFAs in terms of material wealth and plain discrimination in treatment during social interactions began to surface in public spaces. The language was acerbic; the facial expressions were portraits of contempt.[2] The battle was enjoined at multiple levels. Native youths, light-footed and ubiquitous in the society, became self-appointed emissaries of the new war, as it were, to demand respect for their parents and to ensure equity of wealth for their parents and in essence for themselves.

Over time, though, native youths and WFA youths began to work in tandem. This situation was true much later, especially at the nation's institutions of higher education. This situation was rooted in the reality that in most instances, young people rarely carry the grief baggage of a previous generation. They are likely capable of opening up to new ideas. There was an understanding that it was appropriate to lift the mass poor to even a minimum level of comfort. The semblance of that reality was present in the ranks of the doyens of youth activism. Those who otherwise would have passed for children of WFAs were already mixing with children of the indigenes. Their common cord was the education they had acquired from abroad which was driving their mission of alleviating poverty in the country and ensuring economic equality and political fair play. Here, it was becoming a little clearer that paying attention to young people would eventually pay off.

What would that mean? It would mean strong intergenerational dialogue and conversation. It would help ameliorate tension—if the process of intermingling was guided well. It would compel a reexamination of old ideas, which would lead to the emergence of new ideas. It would force society to create rooms all the time, finding spaces, every now and then, to laugh at human foibles. Sometimes adults in society forget a time they were babies, toddlers, and adolescents. They forget the words of scripture: "Out of the mouth of babes and sucklings" comes wisdom.

Indeed, the role of young people in national development is to increase the possibility of alternative perspectives, to loosen needless rigidity that may lead to perdition.

Chapter Four: Notes

[1]Those freedoms (of expression, assembly, etc.) form the bedrock of the mythology of the United States of America being, as it were, the paradise of freedoms, thus, drawing people from virtually all regions of the world. President Franklin Delano Roosevelt's celebrated speech on what he called the four freedoms—freedom of speech and expression, freedom of worship, freedom from want, and freedom from fear—is another piece of political literature of interest.

[2]For the contemptuous treatment of the indigenes by numerous WFAs, see Catherine Reef's *This Our Dark Country*, for example, at pp. 44-45.

CHAPTER FIVE

State Power and Student Activism

STATE POWER IS A CONCEPT which also goes by the name of state rights or rights of a country. State power facilitates the state or country to remain a dominant force over its people. It is all about the set of prerogatives a country, through a fusion of ideas from its people, ascribes by its constitution and sundry laws to watch over its border posts, and the social, economic, political, and religious interactions of its people in ways that ensure peaceful co-existence.

You see, as earlier indicated, the nation-state, Liberia, in West Africa, began, in the 1800s, specifically in the 1820s. Former slaves from the British side of the world had been settled in Sierra Leone, giving Americans an idea to begin settling some of their former slaves also in Africa to ease the burgeoning populations in the country that seemed to have no use for them.[1] A few influential men[2] huddled together to evolve the plan. They would establish some legal entity called the American Colonization Society, draw funds from willing, wealthy

Americans and the United States government, and then embark upon ferrying former slaves and their descendants from the United States, and by that scheme whittle down the threat which the ex-slaves seemed to pose on the white establishment.

First, it would be on the basis of volunteerism, that is people willing to emigrate to Africa. Next, it would be on the basis of holding out a bait—the promise to earn freedom from slavery if a former slave or a descendant chose to emigrate to Africa. And if all else failed, there would be the instigating of laws with an implied threat to send all or most ex-slave Africans back into slavery. This part of the scheme seemed to work, for it sent many scurrying for the next available exit to Africa.[3] The horrors of history will never cease to amaze someone on the chicanery of humanity. How a people that for all their lives had toiled and died in building wealth in a society would get whipped and unceremoniously thrown out of that society without pennies or pants continues to be a sore thumb of history.

The American Colonization Society barreled its way into Africa, scraped land from the Africans met on the Grain Coast,[4] and soon, the Republic of Liberia was born. It took 22 short years—from 1822 to 1847. Power has a way of pretentious plea, and if the response is delayed, it feels justified to foist its own desires. No wonder it is said in the army, for instance, that "a commander's request is really an order." That is the bare-bone story of America's implicit conquest on the Grain Coast where it created an enclave of existence for the repatriated Africans. Howbeit, the modern nation-state was established. Educational activities began. Religious activities began. Political activities were already in full swing. The politics of inclusion and exclusion began, unleashing multiple trendy tensions, six critical themes of which, related to youthful activism, I now highlight and elevate.

Clashes send off sparks. Otherwise, none hears or knows about what transpires in individual communities. That is to say, there may have been controversies—e.g., insufficient school supplies, lunch for students, the treatment of students, affordable tuition, pay for teachers, clean and conducive environment for learning, etc. However, in matters related to the indigenous and WFA sectors of the Liberian population, an early report on brewing conflicts came from the work of Fredrick Starr, an anthropology professor at the University of Chicago.[5] In that work, Edwin J. Barclay who would later become the 18th president of Liberia, but at the moment was serving as superintendent of schools, complained, among other things, about non-compliance of teachers and students with government-initiated educational policies in the leeward regions of the country.

Walling Off "Intruders"—Half or Whole

IN MATTERS OF tension involving youth activism, we come across the first of the six themes of student activism.

Early in the life of the country, the indigenes naturally sought to create a wall against "intruders." On the one side, these people were skeptical of white people, and on the other side, they were skeptical of the WFAs who had settled a part of the land only a few years earlier. Where occasions were possible, they impressed upon "intruders" that they were not welcomed. Whenever indigenous religious and social practices of dance and songs were questioned or denigrated, tensions flared. Whenever these indigenes were treated with contempt, tensions flared.

No to Colonialism or Imperialism

AND WHEN THE era of colonialism or imperialism swept past the era of slavery, particularly after the Berlin Conference of the 1880s, another battle was enjoined. Young Africans, including young Liberians, took up the war of fending off Europe and the United States of America. For example, the French government's attempt to conduct its first nuclear test in Africa, specifically in Algeria in the 1960s, flared up anger among young Africans.[6] Liberian students were in the number, raising issues with the Tubman-led government. Many thought that the reaction of African governments in those days was more muted than what the catastrophe of that incident did require. It should be remembered that by 1960,[7] independent Africa was not as strong as it is today, setting up continental and regional institutions to articulate stances of the continent, talking about west, east, and southern groupings. Waging strong protests against colonialism and imperialism was checkered. The gains of independence made at the time were still being solidified. That reality notwithstanding, African youths were fired up by the spirit of Pan-Africanism which had been energized by the late 1800s, rolling into the early 1900s. Pan-Africanism is the concept of solidarity recognizing one Africa, one African blood, no matter where on the face of the globe.

Yet, in Liberia, the dichotomy of indigenous blood and Western sophistication remained a vexing problem that would exist in stark terms for a very long time. Western education became territorial to the Western-Flavored Africans. When they settled on the Grain Coast among the indigenous populations, their style of education was not embraced—naturally. However, with efforts of white missionaries buttressed by these WFAs over an extended period, the indigenes came into the fold of Western education. This transition produced another theatre of contestation, the first having been the sheer effort to implant African culture with Western culture, a culture espousing different family configurations, different religious rituals, learning configurations, rejection of scarification and sundry practices, etc. So that by the early 1960s rolling into the 1970s, children of the indigenous populations that had been merely sprinkled numbers in the pursuit of Western education rose to a sizeable number articulating matters of equality in the economic and political sharing of the wealth of the nation— its political power and authority, its land, its minerals, etc.

Oral history has it that by the early 1970s, what seemed an idle, snobbish act and voice to denigrate all things indigenous arose during a bout of student politics. An Anderson and a Gobewole were vying for the presidency of student government at the University of Liberia. The former was of the WFA populations, whereas the latter was of the indigenous populations. This native son reportedly placed on a bulletin board his photograph in which he wore his best gown and cap made of local fabric referenced as country cloth. Anderson spoke derisively about why he couldn't understand anyone voting in a "country boy" as president of the student council. Now, from the WFAs' lexicon, "country" had been synonymized with rustic, crude, heathen, and savage.

The derisive remarks almost immediately ignited a passion that would lead to the formation of a distinct student group styled the Student Unification Party, bent on pursuing causes of the ordinary people, the masses, the bulk of whom were the indigenes. These students' focus would become the plethora of political and economic issues rooted in the plight of the working class of the Liberian society. The plight of the poor and ways to ameliorate or completely remove their depressing conditions—e.g., few jobs or no jobs to participate in the money economy that had now taken root in the country, little or nothing for daily, balanced meals, little or no money to send children to school, little or no money to take care of family health needs, little or no money to provide recreation, etc.— would become the centerpiece of their academic and intellectual mission.

The literature of Marxism and sundry philosophies with embeds of socialism and communism as the economic and political salvation of the proletariat or the working class soon became the rallying call. In simple terms, this was the running idea: In a society, people are vested in bonding together to produce material wealth for the benefit of all. But when, in the distribution of the products, laws and sundry systems adversely affect mutual satisfaction, tension naturally rises and everything must be done to stabilize the systems; otherwise, relentless tension will grow. At the center was the interplay of land, labor, and capital. Marx was especially interested in the plight of those who labored to produce material wealth, urging that if they stood cheated, they naturally had to rise to demand just recompense. Thus, was born the tension between work and wages.

Political and Economic Equality Now!

NOW, WITH THE foregoing political development among the young people in college in Liberia, a hornet's nest was shaken. The reality of minority rule in the country, with comparatively few people gorging the wealth of the nation, became a part of the front-end conversation. Year in and year out, the SUP talking points never floated devoid of the plight of the working class. The espousing students talked about the cord running through the economic issues of land, labor, and capital. They talked about most people working and few people enjoying. They talked about corruption. They talked about oppression. They talked about the similarities between the rule of the WFAs and Western colonialism and imperialism. They insisted that if Liberia wanted to build a peaceful society, the ruling elite populated by the WFAs had to expand and become more compassionate.

Schools: The Huddling of the Hurting

EVEN SO, THESE young people had grown to the point of helping to join with and speak about school welfare issues, including, at one end, teachers/professors' welfare comprising the quality and consistent delivery of remuneration, and academic freedom, and, at the other end, students' welfare issues comprising sanitation, furniture, feeding, tuition hike, the abuse of corporeal punishment, security, etc.

To that end, student groups, such as the Liberian Students Union (LINSU) and the Federation of Liberian Youth (FLY) evolved. In constant collaboration, these groups worked and even expanded. The 1970s realized watershed moments. For example, between 1975 and

1976, the move by the Board of Trustees of the University of Liberia to dismiss Dr. Togba Nah Tipoteh from the Business faculty of the school led to student uproar. Among other things, he and a few others were said to have been teaching foreign ideology. Those were jittery times in the country. The words of Karl Marx and sundry prophets and advocates against the misery of the masses were being circulated. Phrases, the likes of "monkey work' baboon draw,'" "the poor getting poorer," "the rich getting richer," often spiced up poverty-related themes and discourses.

By the end of the 1960s and the 1970s, poverty continued to metastasize in the country. The cleavages of poverty and wealth in Liberia were now entrenched. The question of what society should do to either eliminate or ameliorate the pangs of poverty continued to rise. Political and economic theories that seemed to be the panacea began to receive new meaning and relevance. The world has been like that. In lean or difficult times, humanity reaches out to the past for tempting ideas that seem to offer solutions.

That was how, for example, moral philosopher Adam Smith released his monumental book *The Wealth of the Nations*. Smith sought, reportedly to offer his ideas intended to ensure "social peace," which in his day was being rattled by competing social and religious interests. Whereas Thomas Hobbes, his contemporary, insisted on the "Absolute State" or the dominant rule of the state to bring conflicts and upheavals under substantive and substantial control, Smith proposed what he called the "commercial society" or "market society" as the panacea. People freely interacting to acquire and enjoy their basic needs with little or no interference from the state would prove beneficial, he opined.

With regard to Liberia, rural Liberia, without a solid network of roads, seemed to reside on a different planet. The movement of goods and services continued at a snail's pace. Unfunded or sparsely funded schools, low-paid teachers, slow circulation of available capital, soaring prices, etc. continued to make life very difficult. In short, any discourse, whether in or outside of the classroom, that touched on the widening gap between wealth and poverty was intolerable among the elite that were about 5% of the entire national population of nearly 2m inhabitants.[8]

Mark you, the very Dr. Tipoteh had done his doctoral studies on the alleviation of poverty. In other words, he'd studied strategies and techniques that a society could constantly apply to reduce poverty. It would not be a surprise that with like-minded activists he embarked on studies and projects seeking to draw innate ways from local individuals in especially rural communities. PUDECO (Putu Development Corporation) and Susuku, Inc. became outgrowths of the endeavor.

As if the solidarity of students with professors in the incident of dismissing Dr. Tipoteh were not enough, tension arose at Cuttington University College over poor student services and an unhealthy academic environment at the school. In solidarity with the school, the University of Liberia Student Union responded by dispatching a team of inquiry. That was in 1977. The inquiry was followed by a series of other meetings until the situation was brought under some control.

In 1978, whisperings of change of guards at the Monrovia City Hall were growing louder. The temptation for testing the political waters of Liberia was getting intense. By 1979, Dr. Amos Sawyer decided to throw in his cap. That incident ignited the passion of numerous college students who now believed that the call for change all over the country was gaining full strength. It seemed an important theatre for testing some of the political theories these gurus of people-centered politics had been preaching. It won't take long before forces and tensions collided, erupting into the much-talked-about rice riot of April 14, 1979. The political stirring having begun, it appeared that the tension would not stop for the next years to follow.[9] The impact of the city-wide rice riot, a nearly ten-year military rule, and over a decade of civil war would be faulted to their earlier activism.

The point is that with the rise of advocacy for social change to ensure economic equality and political fair play in the country, Drs. Togba Nah Tipoteh, Amos Sawyer, Henry Boimah Fahnbulleh, Jr., and Messrs. Gabriel Baccus-Mathews, Dew Mayson, etc., all in their twenties, and therefore categorized as young people, really young adults, became household names. These seemed the doyens of youth activism. Yet, they would in time drink of the hemlock of disdain. Their mission of sensitization, or what Kwame Nkrumah often called "political conscientization," would become an unpardonable evil warranting a blowback. Their attack on needless proprietary opulence of people that were indifferent to the misery of the mass poor of Liberia would be immeasurably attacked by state functionaries. Sometimes Fate seems to connive in convoluting ways that stall human progress. The April 1979 rice march, the April 1980 coup, and the civil war years would adversely impact the mission and the messengers. Engaging with humanity often has its messy parts. Nevertheless, whether in life or in death, those activists would have to draw upon the words of the Greek Gadfly of old:

> One must not cower in fear at what will eventually happen to us all. More important, one must not do anything known to be wrong in order to escape death: it is better to do what is right, regardless of the consequences, than to do what is wrong to avoid what is both inevitable and good.[10]

Of course, in their case, it would be metaphorical death. The situation in which fighting for a just cause is rewarded with all manners of unflattering names must be tantamount to death. Prior to what I'd call their hemlock years, those doyens of social change activism had produced acolytes, a short cyclical roster of which stands as follows:

Best	Keith Neville
Blackie	Siaffa
Clement	Kwame
Coleman	Fatu
Debbah	Wiwi
Dempster	Yallah
Doe	J. Kpanneh
Duorko	Samuel Kpanbayeazee, II
Du	Thomas
Elliot	Swanzy N.
Flomo	Gedemina
Flomoyan	James
Garlawoloe	Ben
Gbobeh	G. Marcus
Gongloe	Tiawan
Herbert	Christian
Kamara	Siafa
Kesselly	Anthony
Kieh, Jr.	George
Kollie	Krubo
Korto	Joseph Z. D.
Kwiah	James
Jlah	Ben
Lavala	Momolu
Massally	Lucia
Mitchell	Abraham
Morris	J. Sogbah

Musu	Gloria
Ngafuan	Augustine
Nimene	Socratez
Nimpson	Irene
Nyan	Chris D.
Quiah	T. Samson
Pajibo	Ezekiel
Pewu	Sumowoi
Richardson	Tonia
Sando	Gabaworsinah
Sayeh	Bloh
Settro	Morris
Sonii	Boimah
Stewart	Hjaimwoina
Tapia	Wuo
Tiepo	Geepu Nah
Toe	Al Gbi
Toe	Chris
Tokpa	Alaric
Wayne	Sando
Weeks	A. Jesus
Wesseh	Conmany B.
Wiah	Sylvester Taplah
Wolokollie	Dusty
Woods	Samuel K.
Worwor	Kpedee
Wylie	Joe
Yarsiah	James

By no means a complete one, the list—spanning from the early 1970s to the early 1990s—needless to say, should send people wondering: What became of these and many other young people of their time? Although some died in sad, if not mysterious, circumstances, there are several more alive today, at home, abroad, plowing paths of their own. Thinking about them, one may pore over the importance of history, including the significance of historical institutions, such as museums and centers of social change, where, their photos or names arrayed, Liberia would explain to posterity the type of sensitized young men and women, many of whom helped stir society in demand for understanding key socioeconomic and sociopolitical causes and finding ways to deal with them. It would really be important to understand whatever life's mission they chose following the battlefields of youth.

In their element of activism, they were what one might call the "orb of becoming." They were the living image of the white multilayered section of an egg, soft tissues lying close together wrapped around the yellow yolk of life. If you intentionally and attentively eat an egg, peeling its thin, tiny layers, one after another, you are likely to feel the compactness of life. Holding the egg, you recognize that it is the orb of becoming, the source of protein, the source of energy, the source of power. In short, in those days, acolytes of "the struggle," as activists often called the movement, significantly felt they rubbed well into one another. There was often the sharing of food and numerous other resources, with little or no thought of ethnic affiliation. The seamless comradeship was often spectacular. A strong, common sense of nation-building rested in the minds of most, if not all, the young people of the time. When will Liberia ever retrieve that unanimous sense of purpose!

Even so, today, where are those young people? What continues to be their enduring mission—material wealth or the continued, genuine welfare of the poor? Or, have they been stung by the words of Mother Pig?

That is all about a fable—how can one ignore the impact of stories in life!—where Baby Pig once asked Mother Pig about its elongated snout. "Child, in time, you shall know." And the years went by. One day they all celebrated the maturity of Baby Pig who'd just had her very own piglets. A few years later, Baby Pig, who'd now become Mother Pig #2, came from the fields very exhausted. The mother looked on and said, "Child, your snout looks elongated!" Mother Pig #2 contracted an epilepsy of laughter. Her mother went walking by. She knew that Mother #2 had gotten the point: Using her snout to plow through roots and dirt in order to feed her young ones, that snout did become elongated.

Maturity, like seashore waves, either slowly or quickly wipes off youthful idealism. Through the rise of age, life brings us into the realm of understanding some of its intricacies—that is the definition of maturity. Indeed, maturity becomes the border between youthhood and adulthood. It is in the land of maturity that humans come to grips with all the seemingly limitless dreams that they as youth cannot easily detach themselves from and want to turn the world upside down for, never at any minute giving an inch for dialogue, for conversation. Someday, it might be interesting to know which comrade[11] of the past years remained an unabated inspiration or a distressful disconsolate and a disappointment.

A strong and productive society thrives persistently based on an unabated flow of men and women who treasure their rise in life, but never forget their fellow human beings, always fighting to help them sustain life through basic necessities by creating sustainable social programs and projects. But when each advocacy cohort of "the struggle" takes flight upon exiting the crippling effects of poverty and looks seemingly with disdain upon the continuing plight of the poor, then there is a colossal danger, because society then drowns when its cadre and caliber of men and women of stellar value and valor dissipate.

Schools: The Dissipation of Solidarity

IF IN THE past misery became the cord that bound the hurting masses—e.g., students and teachers—together, even at the citadel of knowledge, the ensuing years that rolled in bitterness and bloodshed unleashed suspicion and anger. Thus, whereas the precoup and prewar years were characterized by the jollity of camaraderie, the postwar years were characterized by the coloring of "subversion" and rebellion. Thus, hearing about the mud-slinging phenomena involving school administrators, faculty, and students, no one familiar with the past needed to be surprised.

Students were now denouncing school administrators, charging them with greed and neglect. After all, economic hardships were biting deeply impacting academic performance and driving truancy. Indeed, the reality that no one with substantial state power to ameliorate the situation seemed to be responding adequately drew the ire of students in postwar Liberia, and one school administration followed by another fell by the fury of students.

In the end, we all, soon or late, become victims of circumstances. That is our world, the human world.

Meat-Grain Manifesto/ Alliance

ADDITIONALLY, OVER TIME, the 1980s landed a military coup. The era, too, sadly began to rake down many more young people who'd dare challenge the insanity of the excesses of militarism.[12] In January 1982, a group of six college students got arrested and subjected to torture for engaging in student politics, even threatening them with public execution. And then came August 1984 when General Samuel Doe ordered troops on the campus of the University of Liberia, resulting in rape and mayhem. It needs to be remembered that almost immediately following the April 1980 military coup, the People's Redemption Council (PRC) began to promulgate a slew of decrees. One of these was PRC Decree 2 banning political activities in the country, even in academic institutions and among students. Its very first section read as follows: "...[All] political activities within the Republic of Liberia are hereby prohibited except in so far as shall be specifically allowed or directed by the People's Redemption Council."

Accordingly, the years 1980 through 1985 were immensely tension-ridden for especially academia and PRC functionaries. Many students and faculty were either detained without charge, imprisoned and tortured, or even murdered. Eventually, there came a civil war that spanned over a decade, the impact still being felt to date. Yet, the long drive for social, political, and economic equality, which had driven youthful activism in the country cracked into cleavages. What I call a "meat-grain manifesto/alliance" evolved. Today, the quarrel may not be about who is on the side of indigenous populations or those of WFA. Through cross-cultural marriages and sundry amorous engagements and increased rates of literacy on both sides of the divide, the tension about cultural sophistication, which, for over one hundred years of the nation's existence, helped drive snobbery and needless divisiveness, quelled considerably. However, perennial economic problems exacerbated by nearly 10 years of military rule and over 14 years of civil war have continued to mount an assault on the country.

It has now continued to be more about where one's basket of economic perks can be filled. It is about materialism; it is rarely about the values that often sustain a nation—e.g., hard work, judicious spending of public resources, ample restraint on greed, mutual respectability, etc. A society that is consumed by materialism, sycophancy, selfishness, and wholesale corruption is a society that is bound toward ruination. That is the situation Liberia is in today.

In the Samuel Doe era, there were young cadres for Doe; there were others against Doe. In the Charles Taylor era, there were cadres for his rule; there were others against his. In the Ellen Sirleaf era, the same thing; in the George Weah era, the same thing. Nevertheless, there have been slim splinters of the cadres espousing some of the values that throughout the years spoke to our common humanity—respect for human life, respect for the poor and vulnerable among us, respect for the wealth and wealth distribution of each nation, and the judicious use of its limited resources.

The sad thing is that in the postwar years, the efforts of these splinters of cadres have been unimpressive. If you ever heard about, read, or watched the morality play called *Everyman* of the 12 to 1300, indeed in the Middle Ages, you would notice that the allegorical individual was destined to live life well, practicing good habits and doing every upright thing that would provide for a triumphant entry into the gates of heaven at the time of death. However, this character lived life befriending every other attribute of life except good deeds. By the time death came, the insignificant sprinkling of good deeds was not helpful in the end.

That is how weak the activism among most young people has become today. Meat-Grain Manifesto/Alliance has sapped the strength of the collective force that would have remained monumental, ensuring that state functionaries would forever regret any attempt to mismanage any trust placed by the governed into their care. Many young people have joined songs and speeches in which they thump their noses at those who would not join them in gorging the spoils of war and sundry catastrophes.

State Power Comes to Grips with Student Activism

IT MUST BE a certain degree of idiocy, bordering on pathology, that consumes any adult or elder to think that docility is dumbness or that silence is stupidity. In Liberia, for instance, with the advent of student activism, the initial response of state power was mere complacency: "What do those young people know!" Or, when the activism was saturated more with children of the indigenous populations, the response was this: "What do those country people know!" Hyperinflation of one's cognitive abilities carries a deadly danger. It is embedded with snobbery. It is embedded with complacency. Children are not dead logs. Although often seen as creatures that are supposed to be silent, at least that was an earlier perspective, especially in Africa, the truth is that young people's silence or docility was simply driven by the culture requiring silence in the presence of adults or elders, simply as a sign of respect and decorum.

Yet, it needed to be remembered that all along dormant volcanoes do not mean dead volcanoes. Internally, they are inferno mounds. That might be the state of human beings; that might be the state of young people. Young people also may be icebergs, the tips of which are deceptively unthreatening. Any adult worth some salt must recognize that reality.

Pretty much of the earlier years in Liberia, talking about the Edwin Barclay of the 1930s through the early 1940s, William Tubman of the mid-1940s through the early 1970s, and William Tolbert of the early 1970s through the early 1980s, student activism was met with the spontaneous cry: "Find the Maggot!" or "Find the Mastermind!" In fact, some of the elite adults preferred referring to the young people as "jigger fleas," meaning little nothings! These regime heads and their minions often craved to find some insidious character or a group of characters bent on "soiling the innocent nature" of young people.

This twisted way of thinking about young people must have incensed Dr. Amos Sawyer, one of the doyens of activism in the land, when he made a submission in these words following the rice riots of April 1979:

> I am trying to make two points here, Mr. Chairman: first, given these realities [e.g., Government's indecisiveness to keep possible hiking of the price of rice floating, in spite of the very low salaries of public servants], the question of a possible increase in the price of rice should not have even been entertained. Not only did Government entertain the question, it was in the process of giving it a serious consideration. The second point here is that given these realities, any group—the Association of Liberian Morons, Amalgamated Infants, Inc. (if there were any such groups)—could have mobilized the Liberian people to bring pressure on Government not to increase the price of rice. By considering such an increase and by further permitting such a decision to linger, Government provided the fuel to ignite the fire. No conspiracy was necessary, no acts of treason needed to be contemplated. And even if the so-called 'wicked' used the developments for their selfish designs, was it not Government who created the conditions and nurtured the issue that could be used?[13]

Such responses underestimating the cognitive and emotive abilities of young people highlighted the presumed imbecility of young people/students. Young people/students presumably do not absorb information. Students presumably are ducks. Information like water is poured on them but no drop seemingly sticks. Yet, the reality is that students may not absorb information at the rate that each teacher/professor wishes. But at their very own pace and time, they absorb much of the information fed to them. After all, they are humans with brains, with the capacity for absorption and reflection.

The relevance and significance of Child Psychology and Early Childhood Education must not be trivialized. These fields of study highlight and elevate the evolution of the cognitive and emotive abilities of human beings, from infancy to adolescence. There are numerous facets of adulthood thoughts, attitudes, mannerisms, and behaviors that spring from the underpinnings of life. Understanding the foregoing fundamental realities will accelerate the leadership capacity of a country to provide enormous support to all stages of life.

Finally, with the explosion of information technology, with the increase in cultural mergers and spread, the typical youth on whatever continent has become of an extraordinary character. Thus, even in tiny bits, the child absorbs complex concepts. Accordingly, society should find ways of opening up to young people the storehouse of knowledge regarding every meaningful subject that underlies critical decision-making protocols of life—e.g., sex, family life, health literacy, financial literacy, civic education regarding not only expectations from each national government but also regarding mutual duties of everycitizen for the enormous growth and progress of each nation in the world.

Chapter Five: Notes

[1]Aaron O'Neil's "Black and Slave Population in the United States 1790-1880," at https://www.statista.com/statistics/1010169/black-and-slave-population-us-1790-1880/, placed the figures prior to the American civil war at 4.4 million of the African American population.

[2]These men of influence who helped initiate the American Colonization Society included Robert Finley, Samuel Mills, James Monroe, Bushrod Washington, Andrew Jackson, Francis Scott Key, and Daniel Webster. Among them were clergy, federal government officials, and prominent lawyers. See *New World Encyclopedia*'s "American Colonization Society," https://www.newworldencyclopedia.org/entry/American_Colonization_Society. Also, see Amos Sawyer's *The Emergence of Autocracy in Liberia.*

[3]See the Fugitive Slave Acts. These were laws promulgated, beginning in 1793 and enhanced in 1850 owing to mounting insistence to abrogate such laws. The laws approved the seizing and returning of slaves that dared to escape from their masters. See "What Were the Fugitive Slave Acts," https://www.history.com/topics/black-history/fugitive-slave-acts.

[4]A story of threats and arms-twisting by US naval officer, Robert Stockton, and his accomplice Eli Ayres led to the acquiring of the initial land settled by the Western-Flavored Africans who'd emigrated from America to the Grain Coast in West Africa. The vignettes of land purchases in the ACS saga have been among some of the disconcerting chapters of Liberian history. See Charles H. Huberich's *Political and Legislative History of Liberia* in 2 volumes, Gregg Mitman's *Empire of Rubber: Firestone's Scramble for Land and Power in Liberia,* and Nagbe's *A Nation of Plenty Plenty People: The Liberian Story.*

[5]Regarding that story of tension related to Edwin Barclay's tenure as superintendent of schools in Liberia, *see Liberia: Description, History, Problems* by Frederick Starr. Starr's book details several other interesting aspects of Liberia that should be worth a reading while. For example, he speaks to Liberians' obsession with "government jobs" as an outlet to earn easy income, while government always remains a big loser.

[6]The France nuclear test in Africa stirred an uproar, especially among the young people of West Africa. See the BBC article titled "France-Algeria Relations: The Lingering Fallout from Nuclear Tests in the Sahara," at https://www.bbc.com/news/world-africa-56799670.

[7]By 1960, about 30 countries had reportedly gained independence on the continent. See https://www.thoughtco.com/chronological-list-of-african-independence-4070467.

[8]On the tension of minority versus majority rule in Liberia, see Fahnbulleh's edited seminal work on social change tension in Liberia of the 1970s— *Voices of Protests: Liberia on the Edge, 1974-1980.*

[9]Ibid.

[10]Regarding the quote attributed to Socrates, the old Greek Gadfly, see Bart Ehrman's *Heaven and Hell: A History of the Afterlife*, p. 30.

[11]The books, *Liberia: A Promise Betrayed* and *Christianity and Politics in Doe's Liberia* offer significant insights into student-related treatment in the military era in Liberia.

[12]"Comrade"—every activity has its own vocabulary. The espousal of socialism and communism among young Liberian progressives seemed to require distinctive markers, one of which was to refer to espousers of those politico-economic systems as comrades. Thus, particularly in those 1970 years, each student in the "struggle" responded to "comrade."

[13]For the Sawyer statement about the insanity of wrong causations, see p. 294 of the Fahnbulleh-related book, *Voices of Protests.*

CHAPTER SIX

Summary and Conclusions

I HAVE TRIED IN THIS preliminary short work of creating harmony among the various stages of life in Liberia to lay out key themes of student activism as a way, first, of highlighting them in ways I had not seen them done, especially in Liberia. Hopefully, what I have identified will inspire more elaborate work at multiple levels. I looked at what the earlier approach to youthhood was—discounting their worthiness—and what it must now become: to see them as worthy of genuine respect and consultation in the process of building the nation. The cognitive abilities of every human being are pretty much the same. The dividing line might be one of increments, that is to say, how each age level absorbs the requisite share of cognitive abilities might be different. Just as we slowly evolve, so does the absorption of knowledge. If this one lesson is imbibed, respect throughout the stages of life will not be contested; it will remain automatic and help produce and sustain a harmonious society.

Accordingly, it would be appropriate for every society to provide support and resources in these following ways:

- Invest in understanding people's cognitive abilities.
- Invest in numerous growth and guidance programs and projects.
- Invest in intergenerational dialogues and conversations.
- Invest in intercultural dialogues and conversations.
- Invest in national theatrical and sundry projects.
- Invest in reading programs, the arts, sports, and sciences.

By pursuing each recommendation or a combination thereof, substantive understanding and peace will visit each human shore, including that of Liberia.

Selected References

"American Colonization Society." *New World Encyclopedia*. Retrieved from https://www.newworldencyclopedia. org/entry/American_Colonization_Society.

Berkeley, Bill. editor. *Liberia: A Promise Betrayed: A Report on Human Rights*. Lawyers Committee on Human Rights, 1986.

Crossman, Ashley. "Folkways, Mores, Taboos, and Laws." Retrieved from ThoughtCo, Feb. 16, 2021, thoughtco. com/folkways-mores-taboos-and-laws-3026267.

Drew, Chris. "The 4 Types of Norms (Folkways, Mores, Taboos & Laws)." Helpful Professor, Feb. 17, 2023, https://helpfulprofessor.com/types-of-norms.

Ehrman, Bart D. *Heaven and Hell: A History of the Afterlife*. Oneworld Publications, 2020.

Evans, Steve. "The Impact of Cultural Folklore on National Values: A Preliminary Study with a Focus on Bhutan." Retrieved from Himalaya.socanth,cam.ac.uk.

Fahnbulleh, Henry B., editor. *Voices of Protest: Liberia on the Edge, 1974-1980*. Universal Publishers, 2005.

"France-Algeria Relations: The Lingering Fallout from Nuclear Tests in the Sahara." Retrieved from https:// www.bbc.com/news/world-africa-56799670.

Gifford, Paul. *Christianity and Politics in Doe's Liberia.* Cambridge University Press, 2002.

Huberich, Charles. *The Political and Legislative History of Liberia.* 2 vols. Lawbook Exchange, Ltd., 2010.

Mitman, Greg. *Empire of Rubber: Firestone's Scramble for Land and Power in Liberia.* The New Press, 2021.

Nagbe, K-Moses. *A Nation of Plenty Plenty People: The Liberian Story.* Pentina Publishers, Inc., 2022.

—. "The Mind and the Manner of Productive, Democratic Governance: How the Arts Fit in." Retrieved from https://independent.academia.edu/KNagbe.

—. *Beyond Buffoonery: Exploring Ways to Get Liberia Well-Rooted in All Things Diligent and Dignifying.* Pentina Publishers, 2023.

O'Neil, Aaron. "Black and Slave Population in the United States 1790-1880." Retrieved from https://www.statista.com/statistics/1010169/black-and-slave-population-us-1790-1880/

Quenum, Olmeta. "African Traditions and Customs: Scarification as a Mark of Cultural Identity." Retrieved from https://www.afro-impact.com/en/african-traditions-and-customs-scarification-as-a-mark-of-cultural-identity/

Reef, Catherine. *This Our Dark Country: The American Settlers of Liberia.* Clarion Books, 2002.

Sawyer, Amos. *The Emergence of Autocracy in Liberia: Tragedy and Challenge.* Institute for Contemporary Studies, 1992.

Starr, Frederick. *Liberia: Description, History, Problems.* Retrieved from https://www.gutenberg.org/ebooks/54542

Zinsser, William. *On Writing Well.* Harper-Collins Publishers, Inc., 2001.

www.ingramcontent.com/pod-product-compliance
Lightning Source LLC
Chambersburg PA
CBHW070435290526
45791CB00005B/1984